DUAL CITIZENSHIP

LIVING AS A CHRISTIAN IN AMERICA

GROUP BIBLE STUDY

WRITTEN BY Curtis Ferrell

RELEVANCE SERIES

warner press

Dual Citizenship: Group Bible Study

Written by Curtis Ferrell

Requests for information should be sent to:
Warner Press Inc.
P.O. Box 2499
Anderson, IN 46018
www.warnerpress.org

Kevin Stiffler • Editor
S. Katie Miller • Layout & Design

CONTENTS

The Warner Press *Relevance* Group Bible Studies provide intriguing examinations of topics using the whole of the Scriptures. The guides incorporate various stories and activities to introduce and apply the subject matter, with a Bible study component at the heart of each session. Our goal is to show life-long believers and those new to the faith how to know the Lord intimately while encouraging them to step out and join him in his work with miraculous results.

These flexible studies are ideal for any setting. We know that time is a valuable commodity in today's society, and that's why each book consists of five or six short lessons intended to meet the group's scheduling needs.

"I do not believe that the Constitution
was the offspring of inspiration,
but I am as perfectly satisfied that the
Union of the States, in its form and adoption,
is as much the work of a Divine Providence
as any of the miracles recorded
in the Old and New Testament."[1]

—Benjamin Rush,
signer of the Declaration of Independence

Introduction

This study assumes several premises to be fundamentally true. The person who takes issue with one or more of these premises will likely have difficulty with concepts found in the study. The goal of this study is not to provide an opportunity for argument or partisan debate. However, for those seeking truth and a deeper understanding of our dual role as citizens of both God's kingdom and the United States of America, you may find yourself pondering new ideas about how to approach civil and political engagement.

That being said, here are the foundational premises from which we will begin:

- Human beings are free moral agents—each person has free will and each person is responsible for his or her actions.
- God expects his followers to positively impact the culture around them and to advance the kingdom of God and Kingdom principles.
- God is concerned with and active in current world events, but these events are not so "set in stone" that there is nothing we as human beings can do to change the future.
- The primary concern of God is for the eternal destination of souls, but he is also concerned with all of creation—including how we live in community.
- Christ-followers in the United States bear a responsibility for how their nation is governed and have significant power to determine how it is governed—more so than most of the rest of the world throughout most of history.

Our study will be grounded in the Scriptures. God's Word is our starting and ending point:

> In the beginning was the Word, and the Word was with God, and the Word was God. He was with God in the beginning. Through him all things were made; without him nothing was made that has been made. In him was life, and that life was the light of all mankind.
> —John 1:1–4

> All Scripture is God-breathed and is useful for teaching, rebuking, correcting and training in righteousness, so that the servant of God may be thoroughly equipped for every good work.
> —2 Timothy 3:16–17

The goal of every serious Bible study should not be to simply know the Scriptures, but to apply them. The application of God's Word should always be done within context. In this case, we will be applying the Scriptures to the lives of believers who are also United States citizens.

The United States of America occupies a unique place in history. It was birthed within the hearts and minds of a people who desired, among other things, to worship God as their conscience dictated—a conscience that was informed and shaped by the Bible. We will be looking specifically at that culture and how the founders understood the Scriptures. It will also be necessary to study the concepts of the human will and authority, and basic forms of governance.

This study is designed to be completed and experienced as a group rather than on an individual basis. As a wise pastor named R. Eugene Sterner once said, "God leads his people together." The Holy Spirit has been given to us to lead us on this quest for truth:

> "When he, the Spirit of truth, comes, he will guide you into all the truth. He will not speak on his own; he will speak only what he hears, and he will tell you what is yet to come." —John 16:13

These five weeks of study will include passages from the Scriptures and offer one perspective on what those passages mean to followers of Christ. There are Discussion Questions given at the end of each lesson. Depending on the time available and the nature of your group, you might discuss the Personal Questions as well.

During this study, you will be wrestling with ideas found in God's Word, those expressed in the writings of the founders of the United States, and also those that come from the leading of the Holy Spirit. Share your thoughts, impressions, convictions, and insights freely with the group. Ask questions of yourself, of one another, and of God.

Curtis Ferrell
New Castle, Indiana
January 2019

1. To Elias Boudinot on July 9, 1788, from *Letters of Benjamin Rush*, Vol. I, L. H. Butterfield, ed. (American Philosophical Society, 1951), 475.

L1

Where Do We Start?

All authority flows from God. Some authority was given to humankind.

If we are to properly understand government, we must understand authority. Some people view authority in a way that discounts God's role and can be boiled down to the popular phrase "Might makes right." In this view, authority resides with the strongest group or person. If you can use force to gain control, then you have authority.

In the biblical view, all authority rests in and flows from God:

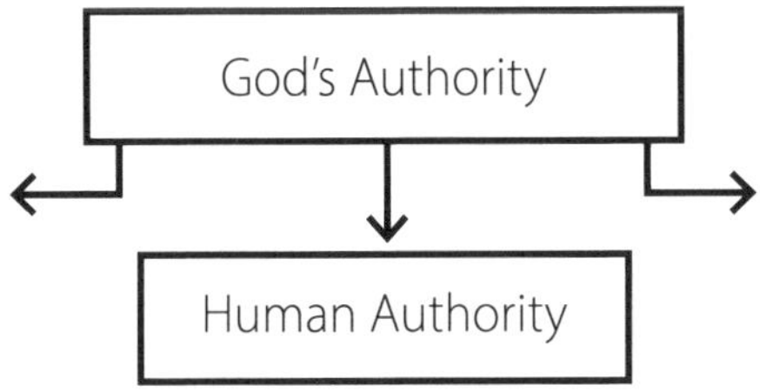

By definition, if God is God then he is all-knowing, all-powerful, and always present, and he is the ultimate authority in the universe. If these things are not true, then he is something less than God.

God delegates, or invests, his authority in others, such as angels and human beings:

> "See, I am sending an angel ahead of you to guard you along the way and to bring you to the place I have prepared. Pay attention to him and listen to what he says. Do not rebel against him; he will not forgive your rebellion, since my Name is in him."—Exodus 23:20–21

> "As the Father has life in himself, so he has granted the Son also to have life in himself. And he has given him authority to judge because he is the Son of Man."—John 5:26–27

> [Jesus] appointed twelve that they might be with him and that he might send them out to preach and to have authority to drive out demons. —Mark 3:14–15

Why do we exist? God made humankind as the pinnacle of his creation. His purpose was that we would be fruitful, that we would multiply, that we would rule over the rest of creation and care for it to the glory of God.

A part of our being fruitful and multiplying is to rule, govern, or steward God's creation:

> God said, "Let us make mankind in our image, in our likeness, so that they may rule over the fish in the sea and the birds in the sky, over the livestock and all the wild animals, and over all the creatures that move along the ground."
>
> So God created mankind in his own image,
> in the image of God he created them;
> male and female he created them.

> God blessed them and said to them, "Be fruitful and increase in number; fill the earth and subdue it. Rule over the fish in the sea and the birds in the sky and over every living creature that moves on the ground."—Genesis 1:26–28

> "As for you, be fruitful and increase in number; multiply on the earth and increase upon it."—Genesis 9:7

> Has not the one God made you? You belong to him in body and spirit. And what does the one God seek? Godly offspring. So be on your guard, and do not be unfaithful to the wife of your youth. —Malachi 2:15

To *steward* something is to care for it on behalf of its owner, and to do so in the way the one who has given it desires. For believers, stewardship is more than just giving money to the church, or how money is used by the church. It is a key responsibility for all of God's children, applying to all areas of life:

> Each of you should use whatever gift you have received to serve others, as faithful stewards of God's grace in its various forms. —1 Peter 4:10

> "[The kingdom of heaven] will be like a man going on a journey, who called his servants and entrusted his wealth to them. To one he gave five bags of gold, to another two bags, and to another one bag, each according to his ability. Then he went on his journey. The man who had received five bags of gold went at once and put his money to work and gained five bags more. So also, the one with

two bags of gold gained two more. But the man who had received one bag went off, dug a hole in the ground and hid his master's money.

"After a long time the master of those servants returned and settled accounts with them. The man who had received five bags of gold brought the other five. 'Master,' he said, 'you entrusted me with five bags of gold. See, I have gained five more.'

"His master replied, 'Well done, good and faithful servant! You have been faithful with a few things; I will put you in charge of many things. Come and share your master's happiness!'

"The man with two bags of gold also came. 'Master,' he said, 'you entrusted me with two bags of gold; see, I have gained two more.'

"His master replied, 'Well done, good and faithful servant! You have been faithful with a few things; I will put you in charge of many things. Come and share your master's happiness!'

"Then the man who had received one bag of gold came. 'Master,' he said, 'I knew that you are a hard man, harvesting where you have not sown and gathering where you have not scattered seed. So I was afraid and went out and hid your gold in the ground. See, here is what belongs to you.'

"His master replied, 'You wicked, lazy servant! So you knew that I harvest where I have not sown and gather where I have not scattered seed? Well then, you should have put my money on deposit with the bankers, so that when I returned I would have received it back with interest.

"'So take the bag of gold from him and give it to the one who has ten bags. For whoever has will be given more, and they will have an abundance. Whoever does not have, even what they have will be taken from them. And throw that worthless servant outside, into the darkness, where there will be weeping and gnashing of teeth.'"
—Matthew 25:14–30

Discussion Questions

1. Read Luke 22:24–30. How does God's idea of leadership and authority differ from what we normally see? Have you seen real-life examples of godly leadership? What did that look like?

2. What are some ways you exercise authority (or could exercise it) in your life?

3. If someone were to examine your life, in what ways would there be evidence that you have "been fruitful"?

4. Other than raising your own children, how could you produce "godly offspring"? (Hint: see 1 Tim 1:1–2.)

5. Think about your work, your hobbies, your interests. How could you "put them to work" for the kingdom of God?

Personal Questions

1. What would it take to increase your effectiveness for God's kingdom?

2. What could you change in your life that might make you more fruitful?

3. John 15:1–8 reveals what many farmers already know—pruning produces a more fruitful plant. What is one thing you might prune from your life that could make you more fruitful?

Closing Prayer

Lord God, reveal to us how you are already using the members of this group to be fruitful and advance your Kingdom. Show us things that should be pruned from our lives. Let your Holy Spirit guide us in being better stewards of the resources you have given us. Amen. ■

In a group Bible study, participants can sometimes put their minds on "auto-pilot." It is important to intentionally and actively agree with the one voicing a prayer rather than just listening to it.

L2

How Does Authority Work?

Human authority is divided among four primary realms: Individual, Family, Spiritual (Large-Group), and Civil (Large-Group). Some of these realms are divided up even further. These seats of authority are established to govern individuals within the realms who are not receptive to the concept of "general welfare" and, ultimately, the will of God.

If everyone always did what was right, followed the Golden Rule, was never mean or hateful, and never lied or cheated or stole, the world would be a wonderful place. But we all have a sinful, fallen nature. God established realms of authority to provide for and protect his people. When individuals want to step outside the boundaries that have been placed there for our protection and work against the "general welfare" of a particular realm, the authority of that realm is there to encourage and, if required, enforce compliance with those boundaries.

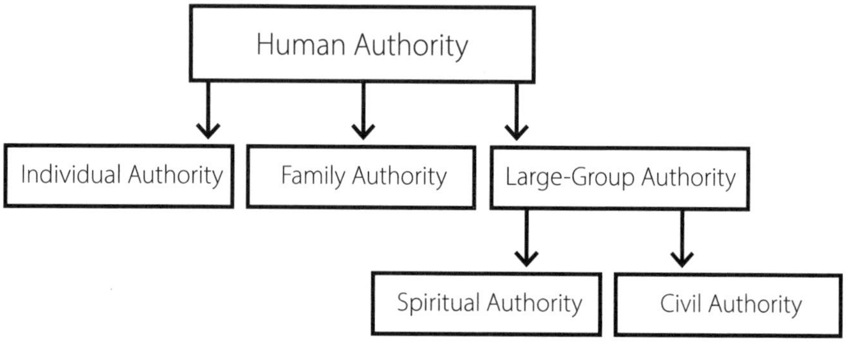

Individual Authority means that we are each responsible for our own choices and have the ability and responsibility to govern our own behavior:

> "If you do what is right, will you not be accepted? But if you do not do what is right, sin is crouching at your door; it desires to have you, but you must rule over it." —Genesis 4:7

> "The one who sins is the one who will die. The child will not share the guilt of the parent, nor will the parent share the guilt of the child. The righteousness of the righteous will be credited to them, and the wickedness of the wicked will be charged against them." —Ezekiel 18:20

Family Authority was established by God to promote the welfare of the family unit, which was also established by God:

> Submit to one another out of reverence for Christ.
> Wives, submit yourselves to your own husbands as you do to the Lord....
> Husbands, love your wives, just as Christ loved the church and gave himself up for her. —Ephesians 5:21–22, 25

> Children, obey your parents in the Lord, for this is right. "Honor your father and mother"—which is the first commandment with a promise—"so that it may go well with you and that you may enjoy long life on the earth."
>
> Fathers, do not exasperate your children; instead, bring them up in the training and instruction of the Lord. —Ephesians 6:1–4

The point here is to illustrate the fact that God has established authority within the realm of the family and not to debate how women's and men's specific roles relate to each other in the home or in the church.

Large-Group Authority involves groups larger than the family, groups that are not necessarily formed by blood. Sometimes these groups are entered voluntarily (e.g., a service club or a neighborhood watch group) and sometimes involuntarily (e.g., students in a grammar school or members of a jury). Two primary divisions within this category are Spiritual Authority and Civil Authority.

Spiritual Authority flows through Christ and benefits the body of Christ (the church):

> Jesus came to them and said, "All authority in heaven and on earth has been given to me." —Matthew 28:18
>
> Christ himself gave the apostles, the prophets, the evangelists, the pastors and teachers, to equip his people for works of service, so that the body of Christ may be built up until we all reach unity in the faith and in the knowledge of the Son of God and become mature, attaining to the whole measure of the fullness of Christ. —Ephesians 4:11–13

> Have confidence in your leaders and submit to their authority, because they keep watch over you as those who must give an account. Do this so that their work will be a joy, not a burden, for that would be of no benefit to you. —Hebrews 13:17

One way to understand spiritual authority is through the following roles:

- Prophets—those who speak to the people on behalf of God.
- Priests—those who speak to God on behalf of the people.
- The Church—those redeemed by Christ, filled with God's Spirit, serving the world, and discipling others. In a sense, all believers now function as prophets and priests.

Civil (or Governmental) Authority promotes the welfare of those who are part of a particular nation, state, city, or other civil division:

> Let everyone be subject to the governing authorities, for there is no authority except that which God has established. The authorities that exist have been established by God. Consequently, whoever rebels against the authority is rebelling against what God has instituted, and those who do so will bring judgment on themselves. For rulers hold no terror for those who do right, but for those who do wrong. Do you want to be free from fear of the one in authority? Then do what is right and you will be commended. For the one in authority is God's servant for your good. But if you do wrong, be afraid, for rulers do not bear the sword for no reason. They are God's servants, agents of wrath to bring punishment on the wrongdoer. Therefore, it is necessary to submit to the authorities, not only because of possible punishment but also as a matter of conscience.

> This is also why you pay taxes, for the authorities are God's servants, who give their full time to governing. Give to everyone what you owe them: If you owe taxes, pay taxes; if revenue, then revenue; if respect, then respect; if honor, then honor. —Romans 13:1–7

> Remind the people to be subject to rulers and authorities, to be obedient, to be ready to do whatever is good, to slander no one, to be peaceable and considerate, and always to be gentle toward everyone. —Titus 3:1–2

> Submit yourselves for the Lord's sake to every human authority: whether to the emperor, as the supreme authority, or to governors, who are sent by him to punish those who do wrong and to commend those who do right. —1 Peter 2:13–14

In the United States of America, civil authority is divided among three branches of government:

- Legislative—this branch of the government makes the laws by which citizens are to abide.
- Judicial—this branch of the government interprets the laws made by the Legislative branch (e.g., What do they mean? How do they apply?).
- Executive—this branch of the government enforces the laws made by the Legislative branch and as interpreted by the Judicial branch.

Discussion Questions

1. Have you ever made a decision you later regretted? What would have helped you make the right decision the first time around?

2. Talk about how you make decisions in your immediate family. Do you make different kinds of decisions in different ways? If so, how and why?

3. When planning a large family gathering (reunion, Thanksgiving, Christmas, wedding, graduation, etc.), who in your family makes the plans? Who gets the final say regarding those plans? Why?

4. In your faith community (local or regional), who wields the most influence? Are final or more significant decisions made by one individual or by a group of leaders?

5. When you think about people who have authority, what are the differences between those who have a "title" and those who have influence?

6. In civil government, there are those who make laws (legislators), those who interpret laws (judges), and those who enforce laws (executives). Which of these three groups has the most authority? Why do you say so?

Personal Questions

1. Have you ever abused your authority? If so, describe the situation. What steps could you put in place to prevent that from happening again?

2. Have you ever regretted *not* exercising your authority? If so, describe the situation. What were the consequences? How might the results have been different if you had stepped up and exercised your authority?

Closing Prayer

God, reveal to us the realms in which we have authority. Show us how to better exercise the authority we do have. Holy Spirit, we ask you to guide us as we submit to others who are appropriately exercising their God-given authority. Amen. ■

L3

What About the Rejection of Authority?

Human beings have been given the gift of free will (self-determination). We can decide whether to agree with, and work within, God's purpose or reject it and go another way. This is the difference between freedom or liberty and anarchy. Free will works independently from authority.

> Going a little farther, [Jesus] fell with his face to the ground and prayed, "My Father, if it is possible, may this cup be taken from me. Yet not as I will, but as you will."—Matthew 26:39

Free will (or self-determination) is a gift from God; by it, we choose how we will respond to authority:

> "If serving the LORD seems undesirable to you, then choose for yourselves this day whom you will serve, whether the gods your ancestors served beyond the Euphrates, or the gods of the Amorites, in whose land you are living. But as for me and my household, we will serve the LORD."—Joshua 24:15

God has given us the freedom to react to authority as we wish. Among the options we have, we can:

- reject all authority.
- submit to some authority.
- delegate some authority (choose others to exercise it).

It was God's original intent to walk with (live in personal intimacy with) humankind, and that is still his desire:

> Then the man and his wife heard the sound of the LORD God as he was walking in the garden in the cool of the day, and they hid from the LORD God among the trees of the garden. —Genesis 3:8

> "I will walk among you and be your God, and you will be my people." —Leviticus 26:12

Instead of communing with God and following his will, human beings chose to live in anarchy (rejecting his authority). The resulting turmoil in our hearts is manifest in the way we live. Our nature is "fallen," and it shows in our attitudes and actions:

> Above all else, guard your heart, for everything you do flows from it. —Proverbs 4:23

> A person may think their own ways are right, but the LORD weighs the heart. —Proverbs 21:2

> The heart is deceitful above all things and beyond cure. Who can understand it? —Jeremiah 17:9

> "Out of the heart come evil thoughts—murder, adultery, sexual immorality, theft, false testimony, slander." —Matthew 15:19

> All have sinned and fall short of the glory of God. —Romans 3:23

Human governance has changed and developed over the course of history. After the loss of fellowship with God in the garden of Eden, governance was family-oriented and became "embryonic"—centered on the rule and will of a patriarch or matriarch, usually the father or eldest living male member of the nuclear family. By Genesis 12, Abram (later known as Abraham) is identified as the first primary patriarch.

Through Abraham's son Isaac, Isaac's son Jacob (also known as Israel), and Jacob's twelve sons and their many descendants, Abraham's family grew to be a "nation" (the Israelites) that would become the primary conduit through whom God would work to communicate his will and ultimately bring salvation. But this was not yet a nation as we might think of it, with consistent national laws and a national identity. Most people's identities were still centered in the nuclear family or the "tribe" of one of Jacob's sons.

After the Israelite nation grew, spent time in slavery in Egypt, and was freed by the hand of the Lord, God gave laws to the people (including the Ten Commandments) by speaking them through Moses:

> When the people saw the thunder and lightning and heard the trumpet and saw the mountain in smoke, they trembled with fear. They stayed at a distance and said to Moses, "Speak to us yourself and we will listen. But do not have God speak to us or we will die." —Exodus 20:18–19

God gave the laws, but Moses served as the judicial authority (interpreting the laws) and executive authority (carrying out the laws) for the Israelites.

Joshua succeeded Moses as leader of Israel, but things soon started to fall apart:

> The people served the LORD throughout the lifetime of Joshua and of the elders who outlived him and who had seen all the great things the LORD had done for Israel....
>
> After that whole generation had been gathered to their ancestors, another generation grew up who knew neither the LORD nor what he had done for Israel. Then the Israelites...forsook the LORD, the God of their ancestors, who had brought them out of Egypt. They followed and worshiped various gods of the peoples around them.... In his anger against Israel the LORD gave them into the hands of raiders who plundered them. He sold them into the hands of their enemies all around, whom they were no longer able to resist. Whenever Israel went out to fight, the hand of the LORD was against them to defeat them.... They were in great distress. —Judges 2:7, 10–12, 14–15

God began to designate judges or deliverers, who ruled by the will of God. As with Moses, they continued to interpret and carry out God's laws:

> Then the LORD raised up judges, who saved them out of the hands of these raiders. Yet they would not listen to their judges but prostituted themselves to other gods and worshiped them. They quickly turned from the ways of their ancestors, who had been obedient to the LORD's commands. Whenever the LORD raised up a judge for them, he was with the judge and saved them out of the hands of

> their enemies as long as the judge lived.... But when the judge died, the people returned to ways even more corrupt than those of their ancestors.... They refused to give up their evil practices and stubborn ways. —Judges 2:16–19

As long as the judge and the people were faithful to God, things went well for Israel.

After some time, the Israelites asked God to provide them with a king—a strong, central leader. This request was actually a rejection of God's "supreme" authority and was the beginning of true civil authority, as provided by a human king, for the people of Israel:

> All the elders of Israel gathered together and came to Samuel at Ramah. They said to him..., "Appoint a king to lead us, such as all the other nations have."
>
> But when they said, "Give us a king to lead us," this displeased Samuel; so he prayed to the Lord. And the Lord told him: "Listen to all that the people are saying to you; it is not you they have rejected, but they have rejected me as their king." —1 Samuel 8:4–7

A king held all three forms of governmental power: he made the laws (legislative), interpreted them (judicial), and enforced them (executive). As with the judges, things went well as long as the king was faithful to God. If the king followed his own will and turned from God or if the people rebelled against the king, the government collapsed or turned evil.

The first king (Saul) quickly failed, the second (David) seemed ideal, and the third (Solomon) did okay, but subsequent kings (and the people) increasingly failed to follow God's will. So God began to send prophets—men and women directly called by God to warn the people about breaking God's laws. Civil authority remained with the king, but spiritual authority now resided with the prophets.

As before, things went well if the people were faithful to God and listened to the prophets. If they turned from God or ignored the prophets, the government collapsed or turned evil. Eventually, the civil side of things fell apart entirely:

> The Lord…sent word to them through his messengers again and again…. But they mocked God's messengers, despised his words and scoffed at his prophets until the wrath of the Lord was aroused against his people and there was no remedy. He brought up against them the king of the Babylonians, who killed their young men with the sword in the sanctuary, and did not spare young men or young women, the elderly or the infirm. God gave them all into the hands of Nebuchadnezzar. He carried to Babylon all the articles from the temple of God, both large and small, and the treasures of the Lord's temple and the treasures of the king and his officials. They set fire to God's temple and broke down the wall of Jerusalem; they burned all the palaces and destroyed everything of value there.
>
> He carried into exile to Babylon the remnant, who escaped from the sword, and they became servants to him and his successors. —2 Chronicles 36:15–20

Throughout history, there have been some who sought to reunite spiritual and civil authority in one ruler. This doctrine is known as the "divine right of kings": a political concept or religious belief in the God-given right to rule. The concept states that a monarch (a king or queen) is not subject to any earthly authority, but rules by the will and authority of God. This means that only God can judge an unjust monarch, and any attempt to remove or restrict the monarch's powers is considered disobedience toward God himself.

History contains many examples of times when people rebelled against authority. Sometimes they rejected spiritual authority (e.g., the French Revolution). And at other times they rejected the civil authority (the king) that had corrupted and usurped spiritual authority (e.g., the American Revolution).

Discussion Questions

1. What are some examples of the benefits of people submitting to authority?

2. Give some examples of times when people abused their authority. In your examples, why was this wrong (what were the offenses)?

3. What are some examples of people not submitting to authority? Was their rebellion justified or not? Explain.

4. When it comes to submitting to authority, is there a difference between driving faster than the posted speed limit and resisting a police officer? Explain.

5. What are some examples (if any) of times when submitting to God's authority would require being disobedient to earthly authority?

6. What is the difference between disobeying authority and undermining authority? Share an example of undermining someone's authority.

Personal Questions

1. Have you ever refused to submit to authority and not gotten caught? Describe the experience. In the eyes of God, were you right or wrong? Why?

2. Have you ever submitted to the authority of someone else, but felt guilty because you violated your conscience? Describe the experience. In the eyes of God, were you right or wrong? Why?

Closing Prayer

God, we pray that you will continue to reveal to us the various realms of authority in our lives— areas where we have been given authority to exercise and also areas where people have authority over us. Help us to exercise your authority with grace and integrity. And we ask your Holy Spirit to correct us when we disobey or undermine those who exercise authority over us. Amen.■

L4

What Was America's Approach to Authority?

"Governments are instituted among Men,
deriving their just powers from the consent of the governed."[1]
—The Declaration of Independence

The civil government of the United States of America is called a Social Compact; it was structured and instituted by consensus:

> "The idea that everyone could have a direct relationship with God and that all were equal before God led to the idea that earthly authorities could be judged and should be judged. If God was the ultimate judge and the Judge above all other judges, then surely each person could consider whether those in authority over him were exercising that authority in accordance with God's principles—or not in accordance with God's principles, which is to say, in a way that could be considered tyrannous. This was an unprecedented development."[2]
> —Eric Metaxas, *If You Can Keep It*

Many people frequently call the United States a democracy. But it is not a "pure democracy," where the simple majority of the people rules. Nations structured as pure democracies eventually consume and destroy themselves. The founders of our nation clearly realized this:

> "Democracy is the most vile form of government.... Democracies have ever been spectacles of turbulence and contention; have ever been found incompatible with personal security or the rights of property; and have in general been as short in their lives as they have been violent in their deaths."[3] —James Madison, Father of the Constitution and Fourth President of the United States

> "A simple democracy is the devil's own government."[4] —Benjamin Rush, Founding Father and signer of the Declaration of Independence

> "Democracy will soon degenerate into an anarchy; such an anarchy that every man will do what is right in his own eyes and no man's life or property or reputation or liberty will be secure, and every one of these will soon mould itself into a system of subordination of all the moral virtues and intellectual abilities, all the powers of wealth, beauty, wit and science, to the wanton pleasures, the capricious will, and the execrable cruelty of one or a very few."[5] —John Adams, Second President of the United States

> "A democracy is a volcano which conceals the fiery materials of its own destruction. These will produce an eruption and carry desolation in their way."[6] —Fisher Ames, Founding Father and framer of the First Amendment to the Constitution

> "Remember, democracy never lasts long. It soon wastes, exhausts, and murders itself. There never was a democracy yet that did not commit suicide. It is in vain to say that democracy is less vain, less proud, less selfish, less ambitious, or less avaricious than aristocracy or monarchy. It is not true, in fact, and nowhere appears in history. Those passions are the same in all men, under all forms of simple government, and when unchecked, produce the same effects of fraud, violence, and cruelty. When clear prospects are opened before vanity, pride, avarice, or ambition, for their easy gratification, it is hard for the most considerate philosophers and the most conscientious moralists to resist the temptation. Individuals have conquered themselves. Nations and large bodies of men, never."[7]
> —John Adams

> "The known propensity of a democracy is to licentiousness which the ambitious call, and ignorant believe to be, liberty."[8] —Fisher Ames

The United States of America is properly defined as a republic (specifically, a constitutional republic)—a form of government in which the head of the state, as well as other officials, are elected by the people to represent them. Rule is by the will of the people, and their representatives seek to build consensus.

In a republic, a charter of rights (in our case, the Constitution) protects certain inalienable rights that cannot be taken away by the government, even if it has been elected by a majority of voters. The reason certain rights are inalienable is because they are "natural rights" or "rights given by God." Many governments try to, and eventually do, remove rights from their citizens that should be inalienable. Inalienable rights are "inalienable" because we recognize that they were granted by God and not the government. As a result, governments cannot (or should not) take those rights away. In a pure democracy, the majority is not restrained by any inalienable rights and can impose its will on the minority.

Even republics can become dysfunctional; but when they do, self-interest and political opposition tend to slow their decline.

The genius of the structure of the United States government is that we are a democratic, shared-power, republic—ruled by the will of the people, but with the understanding that the people are submissive to the spiritual authority of God:

> "Select capable men from all the people—men who fear God, trustworthy men who hate dishonest gain—and appoint them as officials over thousands, hundreds, fifties and tens." —Exodus 18:21

The founders used Isaiah 33:22 as they crafted the U.S. Constitution and separated the federal government into the three branches (Legislative, Judicial, and Executive)[9]:

> The LORD is our judge, the LORD is our lawgiver, the LORD is our king; it is he who will save us. —Isaiah 33:22

The first line of the Preamble to the Constitution begins, "We the People." This statement describes a government that is designed to build consensus in how it operates. It is by consensus that we:

- reserve to ourselves some lawmaking authority. In other words, ballot proposals for laws can be voted on directly by the citizens as opposed to being voted on by representatives.

- elect legislators.
- elect executives.
- created our governmental structure (through the Constitution and its Amendments).

The "American Experiment" is further unique in its structure. Our nation was founded based on the following understandings and restrictions with respect to authority:

- *Personal* authority (the will of the individual) is submitted to God.
- *Local* authority is delegated by the people and is limited; it can be reclaimed and re-delegated. There are checks and balances between local lawgivers, judges, and executives.
- *State* authority is delegated by the people and is even more limited; it can be reclaimed and re-delegated. There are checks and balances between state lawgivers, judges, and executives.
- *Federal* authority is delegated by the people and is the most limited; it can be reclaimed and re-delegated. There are checks and balances between federal lawgivers, judges, and executives.

Personal authority cannot be delegated, although we can abdicate it, in which case it will be assumed or acquired by others. Sometimes people try to usurp the personal authority of others without consent. When the people are no longer submissive to the spiritual authority of God, the church has, at times, tried to reunite spiritual and civil authority in an attempt to avoid anarchy. But the people (who have rejected spiritual authority) also reject spiritual authority when it is united with civil authority.

1. See "Declaration of Independence: A Transcription" at https://www.archives.gov/founding-docs/declaration-transcript.

2. Eric Metaxas, *If You Can Keep It: The Forgotten Promise of American Liberty* (New York: Viking, 2016), 109.

3. See "James Madison" at https://madison.thefreelibrary.com/.

4. Michael A. Shea, *In God We Trust: George Washington and the Spiritual Destiny of the United States of America* (Derry, NH: Liberty Quest L.L.C., 2012), 227.

5. *The Founders' Almanac: A Practical Guide to the Notable Events, Greatest Leaders & Most Eloquent Words of the American Founding,* Matthew Spalding, ed. (Berwyn Heights, MD: Heritage Books, 2004), 148.

6. Fisher Ames, *Works of Fisher Ames* (Boston: T. B. Wait & Co., 1809), 384.

7. Charles Francis Adams, *The Works of John Adams, Second President of the United States,* Vol. VI (Boston: Charles C. Little and James Brown, 1851), 484–485.

8. *Works of Fisher Ames: with a selection from his speeches and correspondence,* Seth Ames, ed. (Boston: Little, Brown and Company, 1854), 349.

9. See "James Madison and the Constitution and Branches of Government" at https://thestoryoflibertyblog.com/2012/06/21/james-madison-and-the-constitution-and-branches-of-government/. Madison is the one who proposed the plan to divide the central government into three branches. He discovered this model of government from what he considered the example of the "Perfect Governor" in Isaiah 33:22.

Discussion Questions

1. In a group of people who come together with a common interest, should it be easy or difficult to find consensus? Why?

2. In a group of people who are selected randomly, is the possibility great or small that they will find consensus? Why?

3. Would it be better to live in a republic where people recognize the authority of God (i.e., where they have a common moral framework and worship the same God) or in a republic where people reject the authority of God (i.e., where they have diverse moral frameworks and worship different gods)? Why? Share what you think each society might look like.

4. In the United States of America, the offices of lawmaker, judge, and executive are held by different individuals. Give some examples of what could happen if two of these offices were held by the same person. For example, what if those who made the laws also interpreted them (legislative/judicial)? What if those who made the laws also enforced them (legislative/executive)? What if those who interpreted the laws also enforced them (judicial/executive)?

5. Short of revolution, what are some ways "We the People" can correct a leadership problem with legislators? with judges? with executives? Which of these solutions require consensus? Explain.

6. How is consensus different from compromise?

7. When the consensus opinion is too close to compromising the biblical principles of a Christ-follower, what is the best way for that person to change the consensus opinion? Can political power move society's point of consensus? Explain.

8. In a particular culture, most issues have a point where consensus can be reached, and this point can shift "left or right" as the culture changes. Do you think the church can move society's point of consensus on any issues without becoming involved politically? If so, how? If not, why not?

Personal Questions

1. What are some issues in society that you would never compromise on?

2. Are there issues that you wouldn't mind compromising on? If so, what are they, and what would compromise look like?

3. William Wilberforce was a British politician who used incremental gains to eventually eliminate slavery in Great Britain. Many "hard liners" in his day believed he was compromising the truth. On those issues where you would never compromise, are there smaller steps or related issues where consensus might be possible? Explain.

Closing Prayer

God, empower us to become consensus-builders and give us the courage to reject compromising biblical principles. We pray for our legislative representatives, our judges, and our executive representatives—mayors, governors, and the President. We ask that you would empower them to serve with integrity. Amen. ■

I
VOTED
TODAY

L5

What Is Our Responsibility?

Followers of Jesus Christ have some powerful and important responsibilities as citizens of God's kingdom who are also citizens of the United States of America.

First of all, it is our duty to pray for those in leadership and for their success as leaders:

> In the LORD's hand the king's heart is a stream of water that he channels toward all who please him. —Proverbs 21:1

> "Seek the peace and prosperity of the city to which I have carried you into exile. Pray to the LORD for it, because if it prospers, you too will prosper." —Jeremiah 29:7

> I urge, then, first of all, that petitions, prayers, intercession and thanksgiving be made for all people—for kings and all those in authority, that we may live peaceful and quiet lives in all godliness and holiness. This is good, and pleases God our Savior.
> —1 Timothy 2:1–3

There is a great guide for praying for public leaders at www.publicservantsprayer.org. It is not affiliated with any political party and covers all fifty states.

Whether or not we agree with the decisions of our leaders, we are not to speak derogatorily against our leaders:

> "Do not blaspheme God or curse the ruler of your people."
> —Exodus 22:28

> Do not revile the king even in your thoughts, or curse the rich in your bedroom, because a bird in the sky may carry your words, and a bird on the wing may report what you say. —Ecclesiastes 10:20

> Ananias ordered those standing near Paul to strike him on the mouth. Then Paul said to him, "God will strike you, you whitewashed wall! You sit there to judge me according to the law, yet you yourself violate the law by commanding that I be struck!"
>
> Those who were standing near Paul said, "How dare you insult God's high priest!"
>
> Paul replied, "Brothers, I did not realize that he was the high priest; for it is written: 'Do not speak evil about the ruler of your people.' "
> —Acts 23:2–5

> Show proper respect to everyone, love the family of believers, fear God, honor the emperor. —1 Peter 2:17

A part of acting as responsible citizens is also to "be fruitful and multiply," as mentioned in Lesson 1. If we have children, we teach them to love God and be good citizens themselves. And whether or not we have any biological children, we are fruitful when we bear *spiritual* offspring by bringing people to Christ and discipling them.

Good citizens understand the different realms of authority and operate within them accordingly. Within each realm (Individual, Family, Spiritual, Civil) there are specific actions we have the authority and responsibility to take. We should be proactive in advancing Kingdom principles wherever we have the authority to act, understanding that all actions are answerable to the authority of God and his Word. Whenever possible, we should seek consensus (in the Family, Spiritual, and Civil realms) while keeping in mind God's gift of free will.

Not only do we exercise authority properly, but we submit to authority as well. Remember, some of your authority has been delegated by you to others or belongs to others as prescribed by God's Word.

If you are required by some human authority to be disobedient to God's authority, you have three choices:

1. Remove yourself from that realm of authority.

2. Resist with civil disobedience. Civil disobedience is being disobedient to the specific "requirement" but still honoring the *position* of authority. If you are civilly disobedient, you will be subjected to the consequences of that disobedience.

3. Agree to the requirement and become disobedient to God.

The ways we exercise our authority and submit to authority constitute acts of stewardship. You have been given many gifts, one of which is the gift of citizenship in the United States of America. You must steward that gift and the responsibilities that come with it:

- Be informed about national, state, and local governing issues.
- Develop relationships with your representatives.
- Go to town hall meetings.
- Write and call your representatives. Encourage them, but also voice your opinion.
- Vote!
- Consider running for office or supporting someone who is running.
- Consider working in, or in partnership with, government.
- Understand what government cannot, or should not, do. For example, the government cannot regulate how, when, or where we can worship, who we associate or meet with, or what we say (verbally or in print or electronic form). These and other "inalienable rights" are reaffirmed in the Bill of Rights. But should the government be able to force clergy to participate in marriages that would violate their conscience? How about requiring us to pay for, or participate in, medical procedures that violate our conscience? How about requiring schools to teach children things that their parents would prefer they not be exposed to?
- In those areas where you have the authority, take the initiative to accomplish what government cannot, or should not, do.

In all of this, remember the gift of free will and how it operates within each realm of authority. Free will means people can choose to either comply with authority or defy authority. This ability—to comply with authority or defy it—is highly valued by God. While it permits the possibility of acting in self-serving and destructive ways, it is the only condition that allows us to act purely out of love, compassion, and gratitude—without compulsion.

The Bible has plenty to say about building consensus:

> Do two walk together unless they have agreed to do so? —Amos 3:3

> If it is possible, as far as it depends on you, live at peace with everyone. —Romans 12:18

> If the unbeliever leaves [a marriage], let it be so. The brother or the sister is not bound in such circumstances; God has called us to live in peace. —1 Corinthians 7:15

> Finally, brothers and sisters, rejoice! Strive for full restoration, encourage one another, be of one mind, live in peace. And the God of love and peace will be with you. —2 Corinthians 13:11

> Acknowledge those who work hard among you, who care for you in the Lord and who admonish you. Hold them in the highest regard in love because of their work. Live in peace with each other. —1 Thessalonians 5:12–13

> Make every effort to live in peace with everyone and to be holy; without holiness no one will see the Lord. —Hebrews 12:14

Consensus is not compromise. There is almost always some common ground everyone can agree on that does not compromise the principles of any of the parties involved. Agreeing with a political opponent does not always equal compromise.

Various people hold different views on a subject—in other words, each person has his or her own "optimal" point of view. As discussed in Lesson 4, most issues have a point where consensus can be reached, but this point will be somewhat removed from the point each person considers optimal. Moving a consensus point closer to your optimal point can only happen by changing the culture of the group seeking consensus. This shift cannot be accomplished politically or by force; it can only occur as each individual moves closer to the same worldview. From the perspective of a Christian, it can only be accomplished as each individual agrees more closely with the will of God.

As Charles Colson wrote, "Christians who understand biblical truth and have the courage to live it out can indeed redeem a culture, or even create one. This is the challenge facing all of us in the new millennium."[1]

1. Charles W. Colson, *How Now Shall We Live?* (Wheaton, IL: Tyndale House, 1999), 477.

Discussion Questions

1. How is praying *at* someone different from praying *for* someone? Is one a more acceptable kind of prayer than the other? Explain.

2. If the Scriptures teach us not to speak negatively against a leader (not to curse, speak evil about, or revile him or her), is there a way to speak against the policies, positions, and actions of a leader while still giving that person due respect? Explain.

3. When we exercise authority, it means assuming responsibility for the outcome of our actions. What are some reasons people shy away from or refuse to exercise authority?

4. What is the difference, if any, between civil disobedience and rebelling against authority? Can you think of an example of civil disobedience that does not honor God? Explain.

5. Citizenship is a gift that God wants us to steward well. What are some other gifts that God expects us to steward well?

6. In biblical examples of stewardship, there is a "return on investment" that the steward is expected to show. What would be a good return on investment if we are effective in stewarding our citizenship?

Personal Questions

1. Have you ever had to make a tough decision about not submitting to authority? What was the struggle, and what was the outcome?

2. In the various "group" realms of authority (Family, Spiritual, and Civil), when the group has needed to make a decision, have you been more likely to seek consensus or to forcefully champion an ideology you consider "pure"? After decisions have been made, did the group experience closer and stronger relationships, or did there seem to be more division and dissention? Why do you think this was so?

Closing Prayer

Lord God, we ask you to reveal all of the responsibilities we have as citizens of God's kingdom, our nation, our community, and our families. May your Holy Spirit guide us as we seek to both excercise authority and build consensus. We continue to pray for our leaders. And we ask you to show us how we can be more fruitful as citizens of the kingdom of God who are also citizens of the United States of America.■

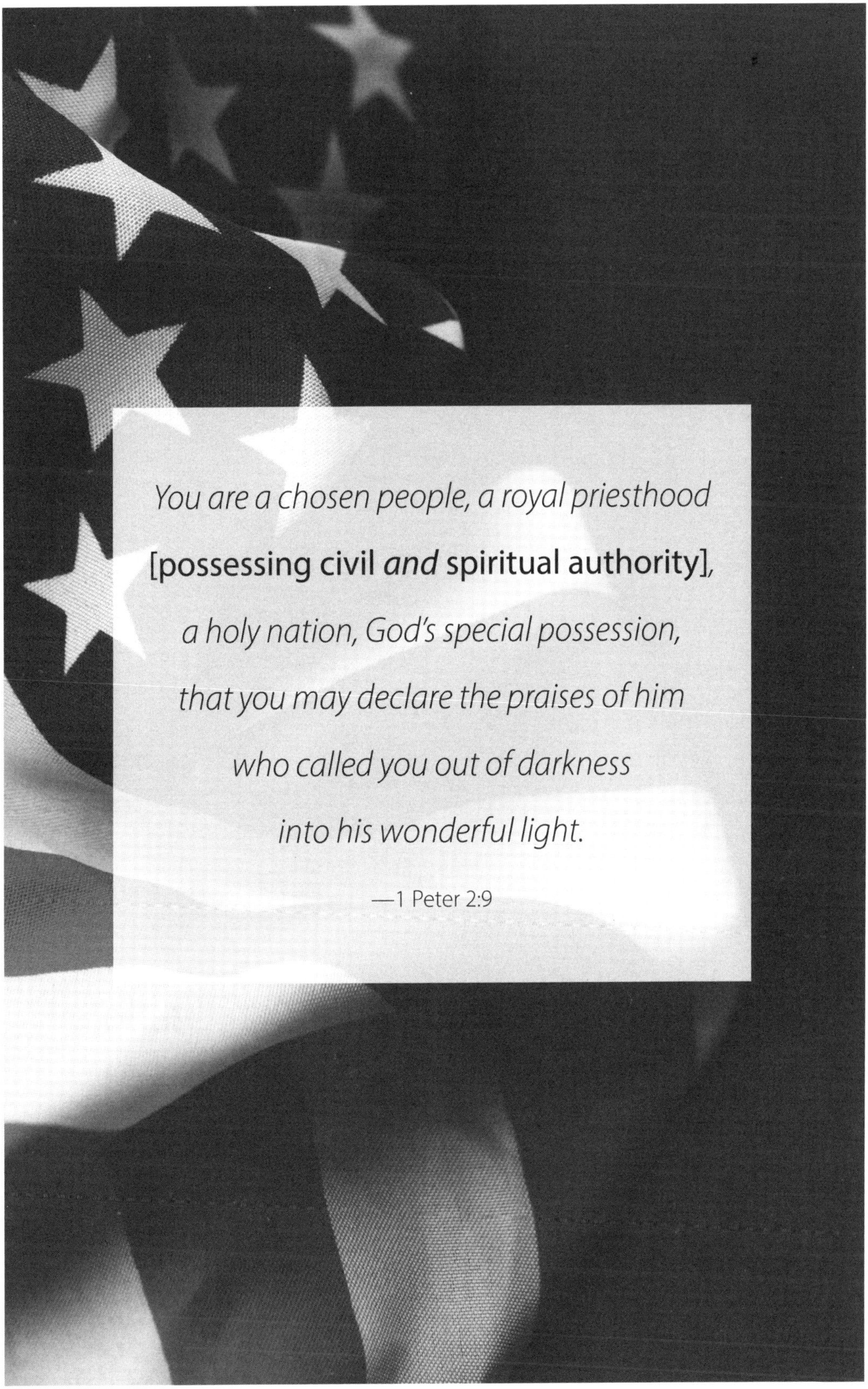

You are a chosen people, a royal priesthood
[possessing civil *and* spiritual authority],
a holy nation, God's special possession,
that you may declare the praises of him
who called you out of darkness
into his wonderful light.

—1 Peter 2:9

The Founding Fathers

The term *Founding Fathers* is often used to describe the group of philosophers, politicians, and writers who led the American Revolution. Here is some brief information on the four Founding Fathers mentioned in Lesson 4.

James Madison (March 16, 1751–June 28, 1836) served as the fourth President of the United States (1809–1817) and as a member of the Continental Congress. He is considered the Founder of the Constitution and the Father of the Bill of Rights.

Benjamin Rush (January 4, 1746–April 19, 1813) was a signer of the Declaration of Independence, a member of the Continental Congress, a physician, and an educator. He helped begin the American Sunday School Movement and helped organize America's first anti-slavery society.

John Adams (October 30, 1735–July 4, 1826) served as the second President of the United States (1797–1801), as the first Vice-President (1788–1796), and as a delegate to the first and second Continental Congresses. He also assisted in drafting the Declaration of Independence.

Fisher Ames (April 9, 1758–July 4, 1808) was a Massachusetts member of the U.S. House of Representatives in the first four Congresses, a member of the Federalist Party, and a school teacher. He was a skilled orator and was not afraid to speak his mind even when in the minority.